Published by Maple Tree Press Inc.
51 Front Street East, Suite 200, Toronto, Ontario M5E 1B3

Text © 2001 Lyn Thomas
Illustrations © 2001 Dianne Eastman

Distributed in the United States by Firefly Books (U.S.) Inc.
230 Fifth Avenue, Suite 1607, New York, NY 10001

We acknowledge the financial support of the Canada Council for the Arts, the Ontario Arts Council, and the Government of Canada through the Book Publishing Industry Development Program (BPIDP) for our publishing activities.

Dedication

To my friend Barbara who lives in Melbourne, Australia, and is one of the most amusing people I know. She made me laugh when we sat together in class and some forty years later she still manages to have me in stitches—even by email. And I would like to acknowledge all the children in the world who continue to recycle all the great jokes and Knock! Knocks! that I heard as a child, and still find them funny. *L.T.*

To Harold, for loving laughter. I would also like to recognize the anonymous engravers and illustrators, of both nineteenth and twentieth centuries, whose fine work has been incorporated into many of the illustrations in this book. *D.E.*

Cataloguing in Publication Data

Thomas, Lyn, 1949–
  Ha! ha! ha! : 1,000+ jokes, riddles, facts, and more

ISBN 1-894379-15-2 (bound)   ISBN 1-894379-16-0 (pbk.)

1. Riddles, Juvenile.   2. Wit and humor, Juvenile.   3. Puzzles — Juvenile literature.
4. Amusements — Juvenile literature.   I. Eastman, Dianne.   II. Title.

PN6371.5.T46   2001   j793.73   C00-932403-8

Design & art direction: Dianne Eastman
Illustrations: Dianne Eastman

Printed in Canada

C   D   E   F

What goes
ha, ha, ha, ha,
plop?

Someone
laughing his
head off!

Ha! Ha! Ha!

1,000+ Jokes, Riddles, Facts, and More

Written by
LYN THOMAS

Illustrated by
DIANNE EASTMAN

MAPLE
TREE
PRESS

4

Thanks for the warning, Thumper!

Remember Bambi's bunny friend, Thumper? Like real rabbits, Thumper tapped the ground with his feet. When rabbits sense danger, they thump their enormous feet, probably so the sound will warn others to be on their guard.

5

Lost in Space

What sport are aliens best at?

Space-ball

What do you call a pan spinning through space?

An unidentified frying object.

What's an astronaut's favorite drink?

Gravi-tea.

Where do astronauts park their rockets?

At a parking meteor.

How do you make a baby sleep on a space ship?

You rocket.

What do space cows say?

Mooooo-n.

Do Astronauts Cry?

An astronaut might feel sad, but it's impossible to cry in space. Why? There's no gravity in space so the tears won't flow.

8

Hang on Tight!

Why don't birds fall off their perches when they sleep? They have handy little tendons in their legs. When sleeping or resting, the bird bends its knees, pulling the tendons really tight. This tightening closes the claws, so they grip tightly onto the branch.

It's raining cats and dogs

Can you tell which well-known expression each of these drawings illustrates?

Hint: The expressions are listed below.

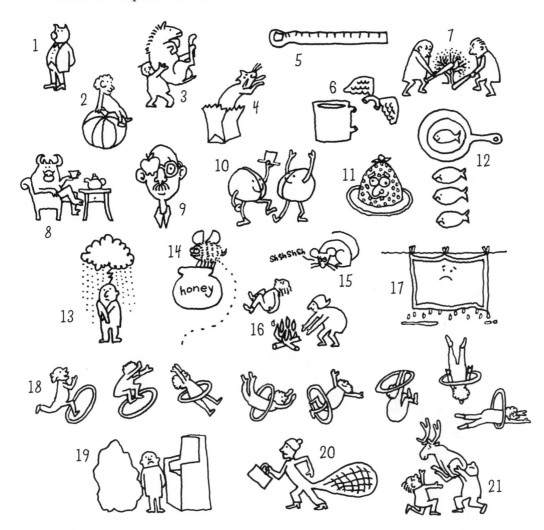

12

A Fishing Cat?

It's true! Most cats hate water, but the Asian fishing cat is a strong swimmer—even underwater! It does catch fish, but is believed to eat mostly snakes, frogs, and crustaceans.

13

Where did the butcher go dancing?
At the meatball.

Which nail does a carpenter hate to hit?
His thumbnail.

Who is the strongest man in the world?
A policeman, because he can hold up as many cars as he wants with one hand.

Why did the girl take a ruler to bed?
She wanted to know how long she'd slept.

What did one geologist say to the other?
Let's go to the rock festival!

Why did the bank customer stand next to the bank vault?
He wanted to be on the safe side.

What did the bald man say when he got a comb for his birthday?
Thank you, I'll never part with it.

What was the newspaper headline when the escaped prisoners fell into cement?
Police arrest hardened criminals.

What would you get if you dropped a piano on an army officer?
A flat major.

What's the name of the world's most famous underwater spy?
James Pond.

How many magicians does it take to change a light bulb?
Only one, but she changes it into a rabbit.

What do people in clock factories do all day?
They make faces.

Who earns a living by driving customers away?
A cab driver.

The Universal Smile

There are thousands of languages spoken and millions of different customs all over the world. But there is at least one thing that all humans understand: the smile. It means the same thing no matter who you are or where you live. Even babies who are blind from birth smile, so it must be a part of human behavior that we know without even having to learn it.

Why did the hairdresser win the race?
She took a shortcut.

How much did the pirate pay for his earrings?
A buck an ear.

Where do kings keep their armies?
Up their sleevies.

15

Picnic Puzzlers

A colony of ants was discovered on the Japanese coast containing an estimated one million queens and 306 million workers in 45 interconnected nests! Bet you'd think twice about throwing down your picnic blanket there!

Where do you weigh a pie?

Somewhere over the rainbow, weigh-a-pie.

What do you get when you cross a skunk with a vegetable?

Smellery.

Why did the cookie go to see the doctor?

He was feeling crumby.

Who tells the best egg jokes?

A comedi-hen.

What did one plate say to the other plate?

Lunch is on me!

What looks like half a lemon?

The other half.

Why did the tomato blush?

Because it saw the salad dressing.

17

Why would you take a pencil to bed?
To draw the curtains.

Did you hear the story about the pencil?
Oh, forget it, there's no point.

What has teeth but can't eat?
A comb.

What did the scissors say to the hair?
It won't be long now.

What do you call a snowman with a suntan?
A puddle.

What did one firecracker say to the other?
My pop is bigger than your pop.

What has wheels and flies?
A garbage truck.

If two's company and three's a crowd, what's four and five?
Nine.

What kind of saw dances?
A jigsaw.

Try saying this three times fast!

Pneumonoultramicroscopicsilicovolcanoconiosis. It's almost impossible to pronounce this word, let alone guess its meaning. Apart from the fact that it's a medical disease, it's also the longest word (all 45 letters of it!) in the Oxford English Dictionary.

What do you know about nitrates?
They're cheaper than day rates.

What did the limestone say to the geologist?
Don't take me for granite.

Who steals the soap in the bathroom?

The robber ducky.

Why would snow and rain make a good bed?
Snow comes in blankets and rain in sheets.

How many sides does a shoebox have?
Two—the inside and the outside.

What kind of ship never sinks?
A friendship.

What goes through a door but never comes in or out?
A keyhole.

What's the difference between a newspaper and a TV?
Try swatting a fly with a TV and you'll find out.

What did the shovel say to the pile of earth?
I dig you.

Where do frogs fly their flags?
Up tad-poles.

Where do tadpoles change into frogs?
In the croak-room.

Where does a frog go to get glasses?
The hop-tometrist.

What happened to the frog's car when it was illegally parked?
It got toad.

What kind of footwear do frogs prefer to wear?
Open-toad sandals.

What's a frog's favorite year?
Leap year.

What does a frog look like when it has a broken leg?
Unhoppy.

What goes into the water green but comes out blue?
A frog on a cold day.

What do you get when you cross a frog with a rabbit?
A rabbit that says 'ribbit.'

What's green and loud and can be heard for miles?
A frog horn.

Why don't you ever see an unhappy frog?
They eat whatever bugs them.

Now that's a great mom!

One kind of poison dart frog goes to great heights for her young. Once the tadpoles are hatched, she carries them from the forest floor to the top of the trees, where she deposits them in the little pools of water that collect in the leaves of certain trees. It's a tough climb, but these are devoted moms.

Knock! Knock!
Who's there?
Police.
Police who?
Police open the door, it's freezing out here.

Knock! Knock!
Who's there?
MT.
MT who?
MT your glass before you take more.

Knock! Knock!
Who's there?
Boo.
Boo who?
Why are you crying?

Knock! Knock!
Who's there?
Dish.
Dish who?
Dish is a very bad joke.

Knock! Knock!
Who's there?
Butcher.
Butcher who?
Butcher can't touch your toes.

Knock! Knock!
Who's there?
Time.
Time who?
Time you got yourself a watch.

Knock! Knock!
Who's there?
Waiter.
Waiter who?
Waiter minute, I'm almost ready.

Knock! Knock!
Who's there?
Lettuce.
Lettuce who?
Lettuce in, and you'll see.

Knock! Knock!
Who's there?
Doughnut.
Doughnut who?
Doughnut open your door for strangers.

Knock! Knock!
Who's there?
Alaska.
Alaska who?
Alaska only once.

Knock! Knock!
Who's there?
Ya.
Ya who?
**I didn't know you were
in the rodeo.**

Knock! Knock!
Who's there?
Carl.
Carl who?
**Carl me back when
you've got time to talk.**

Knock! Knock!
Who's there?
Wooden.
Wooden who?
**Wooden you like to
know.**

Knock! Knock!
Who's there?
Icon.
Icon who?
**Icon tell another Knock!
Knock! joke if you want.**

Knock! Knock!
Who's there?
House.
House who?
House it going?

Knock! Knock!
Who's there?
Acme.
Acme who?
Acme another question.

Knock! Knock!
Who's there?
Anita.
Anita who?
**Anita lot more to eat,
I'm starving.**

Knock! Knock!
Who's there?
Hammy.
Hammy who?
**Hammy a wrench so I
can fix this thing.**

Laugh Attack

Laughs come in all sizes. Whether it's a loud guffaw or an uncontrollable fit of the giggles, laughter has incredible physical effects on our bodies. What exactly happens when you laugh? Around fifteen of your facial muscles contract. When you laugh really hard, you might become weak at the knees, get a stomachache, even shed some tears. Your respiratory system also moves into action. Your windpipe half-closes and you take in air irregularly. Meanwhile, chemical blood sensors tell your body it's running out of air. In response, your heart pumps faster, sending more blood to your muscles. Phew! Sounds like a total body workout!

Laughter on the Brain

Believe it or not, there is such a thing! Gelotology is the scientific name for the study of laughter. Scientists know that parts of our brains are responsible for specific bodily functions. For instance, our frontal lobes are responsible for our emotions. But since we laugh for many different reasons, there's more than one spot on our brains that allows us to do this.

Laugh Facts

Surprise !

If you've ever tried tickling yourself, you know it's impossible. Why? Your brain needs to be tense and surprised for tickling to work. When you try to do it to yourself, your brain is in control and you know exactly where you are going to tickled and what it will feel like. When someone else tickles you, it's a different story. You even react to the thought of being tickled. Your nerves become sensitive in the same way they do when you are excited or afraid.

Funny Funny Bone

The funny thing about your funny bone is that it's not a bone at all. What you're really hitting is your ulnar nerve, the nerve that carries messages to and from your brain and fingers. Most of your nerves are well protected by skin and flesh. But for some reason—and scientists are not sure why—your ulnar nerve doesn't have much padding where it passes through your elbow. So when you bump your elbow, you often hit the nerve, sending a weird tingly feeling to your fingers.

School Daze

How does your eraser erase?

A pencil is made of graphite. When you write on paper, tiny particles of gritty graphite are left on the paper and in the paper fiber. When you rub your eraser across the paper, the rubber picks up the bits of graphite, and like magic, your pencil marks disappear!

Tall Tales *by* A. Lyre

Winter Hikes *by* I. C. Toes

Statues
by Stan Dingstill

Out of Breath
by Ima Puffing

World of Elephants
by L. Ong Trunk

Shell Collecting
by Sandy C. Shore

Be Prepared
by Justin Case

Baseball
by A. Diamond

Credit Cards
by Bill Melater

Watering Hole
by O. Asis

Frisbee
by Iman Orb

GLUE Stick Ing

Dinner Delight *by* Roland Butter

The Contest *by* Willie Winn and Betty Can

The
Contest
by
Willie Winn
and Betty Can

The Haunted House
by Hugo First

What is the only word in the dictionary that's spelled incorrectly?

Incorrectly.

What's at the end of everything?

The letter G.

Which two days of the week start with T?

Today and tomorrow.

What time is spelled the same backwards as it is forwards?

Noon.

What's at the end of a rainbow?

The letter W.

How is the letter D like a bad child?

Because it makes ma mad.

Why is the letter T like a cold day?

Because it's in the middle of winter.

What word becomes shorter if you add two letters to it?

Short.

When do you put the cart before the horse?

In the dictionary.

Which letter is found in a cup?

The letter T.

Which two letters of the alphabet contain nothing?

What has two eyes but can't see?

An icicle.

What's in the middle of America and Australia?

The letter R.

How do you spell hard water with three letters?

What occurs once in a minute, twice in a moment but never in a day?

The letter M.

What 4 letters does the dentist say to her patient?

ICDK
(I see decay).

What has more letters than the alphabet?

The post office.

What's an acronym?

It's a combination of letters or syllables that make a simple, pronounceable word from a series of words. Here are some well-known words: SCUBA (Self-Contained Underwater Breathing Apparatus), RADAR (Radio Detection and Ranging), and LASER (Light Amplification by the Stimulated Emission of Radiation).

Lazy Phrases

Can you figure out these word puzzles? (*Hint:* Sometimes it helps to solve them if you talk out loud.)

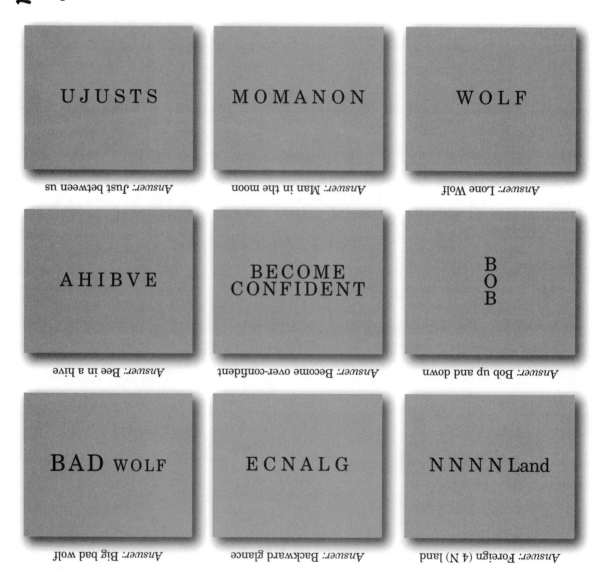

UJUSTS

Answer: Just between us

MOMANON

Answer: Man in the moon

WOLF

Answer: Lone Wolf

AHIBVE

Answer: Bee in a hive

BECOME CONFIDENT

Answer: Become over-confident

B
O
B

Answer: Bob up and down

BAD WOLF

Answer: Big bad wolf

ECNALG

Answer: Backward glance

N N N N Land

Answer: Foreign (4 N) land

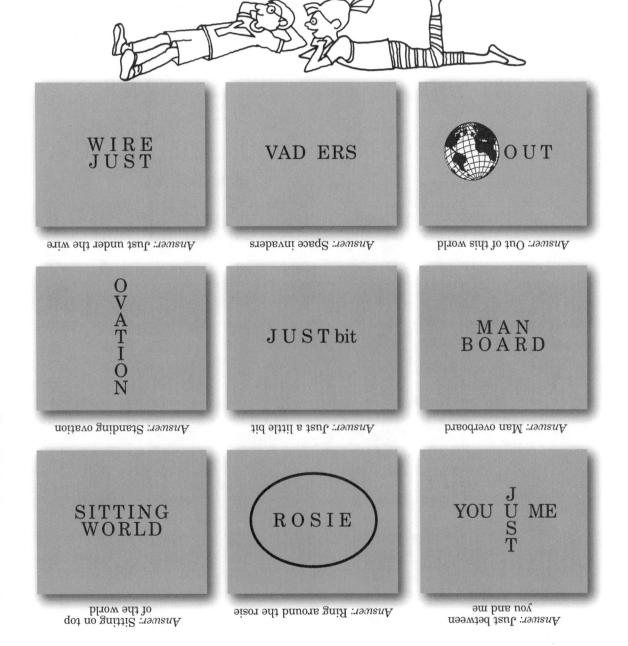

WIRE
JUST

Answer: Just under the wire

VAD ERS

Answer: Space invaders

OUT

Answer: Out of this world

O
V
A
T
I
O
N

Answer: Standing ovation

JUST bit

Answer: Just a little bit

MAN
BOARD

Answer: Man overboard

SITTING
WORLD

Answer: Sitting on top of the world

ROSIE

Answer: Ring around the rosie

YOU JUST ME
J
U
S
T

Answer: Just between you and me

Do You Have Any Earplugs?

Does your dog cringe and try to hide under the bed during a thunderstorm? You might too if your ears were as sensitive as a dog's. A dog's hearing is so keen it can hear thunder long before a person can. If those bangs sound loud to you, imagine how they sound to sensitive canine ears.

All-Purpose Bridge

The Boston Bridge is the only place in the world where you can walk on a bridge, underneath a car bridge, while a train goes over that, while a plane flies above, and boats go underneath.

What did the boy say once he had learned how to count money?
It all makes cents now.

Why did the girl put her money in the freezer?
She wanted cold hard cash.

If a dollar and a nickel were at the top of a tall building, which would jump first?
The nickel, it has less cents.

What's the best way to double your money?
Fold it.

Why did the moon go to the bank?
To get its first quarter.

When does it rain money?
When there's change in the weather.

What's a doughnut?
Someone who's crazy about money.

What has a head and tail but no body?

A quarter.

Big Pengoes

In Hungary in 1946 a bank note was issued for 100 quintillion pengoes, which looks like this: 100,000,000,000,000,000,000.

Is Your Computer Running ?

Why don't fish use computers?
They're afraid of getting stuck in the net.

What do computers eat when they get hungry?
Chips.

Why did the computer sneeze?
It had a virus.

What kind of nightclub did the computer go to?
A disk-o.

Why did the computer have to lie down?
It had slipped a disk.

What did the spider do on the computer?
It made a web page.

Why didn't the computer finish its sandwich?
It only wanted a little byte.

Why do cats like computers?
They like playing with the mouse.

What's a computer's favorite sport?
Surfing.

Why did the computer catch a cold?
It forgot to close its windows.

Why did the computer lose its driver's licence?
It was always crashing.

Why was the computer tired when it got home?
Because it had a hard drive.

How does a computer order food?
Off the menu.

What do you get when you cross a computer with a freezer?
Very cool answers.

snap

Why didn't the computer answer the question?
Because it lost its memory.

Why was the computer good at golf?

It had a hard drive.

43

Computer Terms Glossary!

640K barrier: The finish line in a mega-marathon.
Analog: What Ana tosses into the fire.
Bandwidth: Limited by the size of the stage.
Cursor: Someone who swears too much.
DAT: The opposite of DIS.
Fixed disk: A broken disk that comes back from the shop.
Flat file: A file with all the air out of it.
Home computer: What you tell your computer when it
    follows you to school.
Ink jet: A pen used for skywriting.
Megaflop: The worst movie you have ever seen.
Modem: What the gardener did to the lawns.
Overlay: Chickens making too many eggs.

Smilies

:-)	Smile
:-b...	Drooling
;-)	Wink
=-o	Argh!
:-*	Kiss
{*}	Hug and a kiss
:-(	Unhappy
:-x	"my lips are sealed" smiley
:-c	bummed out smiley
: *>	a cat

Internet Abbreviations

BTW	By the way
HHOS	Ha, ha, only serious
F2F	Face to face (personal meeting)
IMHO	In my humble opinion
FCOL	For crying out loud
IMO	In my opinion
FWIW	For what it's worth
LOL	Laughing out loud
FYI	For your information
OTOH	On the other hand
ROTFL	Rolling on the floor, laughing
HHOK	Ha, ha, only kidding
TAFN	That's all for now

Bugs!

Mark I, invented in 1944, was the first American general purpose computer controlled by programs. In 1945, Mark II was developed, and during its development, a computer term was coined which is still in use today. After a relay in the computer had failed, scientists discovered the source of the problem: a dead moth inside, which had to be removed. This is thought to be the origin of the word "debugging."

Knock! Knock!
Who's there?
A door.
A door who?
**Adorable me,
that's who!**

Knock! Knock!
Who's there?
You.
You who?
Are you calling me?

Knock! Knock!
Who's there?
Weed.
Weed who?
**Weed better do the dishes
before mom gets home.**

Knock! Knock!
Who's there?
Butcher.
Butcher who?
**Butcher didn't think
you'd see me again.**

Knock! Knock!
Who's there?
Watch.
Watch who?
**Watch you want to do
for lunch?**

Knock! Knock!
Who's there?
Little old lady.
Little old lady who?
**I didn't know you could
yodel.**

Knock! Knock!
Who's there?
Isabel.
Isabel who?
**Isabel working or do I
have to knock?**

Knock! Knock!
Who's there?
Turnip.
Turnip who?
**Turnip on time, or you'll
miss the surprise.**

Knock! Knock!
Who's there?
Ice cream.
Ice cream who?
**Ice cream, you scream,
we all scream for ice
cream.**

Knock! Knock!
Who's there?
Must.
Must who?
Must you keep saying that?

Knock! Knock!
Who's there?
Oscar.
Oscar who?
Oscar if she can come out to play.

Knock! Knock!
Who's there?
Aardvark.
Aardvark who?
Aardvark a million miles for one of your smiles.

Knock! Knock!
Who's there?
Francis.
Francis who?
Francis my favorite country in Europe.

Knock! Knock!
Who's there?
Ivana.
Ivana who?
Ivana suck your blood!

Knock! Knock!
Who's there?
Banana.
Banana who?
Knock! Knock!
Who's there?
Banana.
Banana who?
Knock! Knock!
Who's there?
Banana.
Banana who?
Knock! Knock!
Who's there?
Orange.
Orange who?
Orange you glad I didn't say banana?

Knock! Knock!
Who's there?
Henrietta.
Henrietta who?
Henrietta large pizza and didn't share with anyone.

Knock! Knock!
Who's there?
Ima.
Ima who?
Ima tired of knocking, can't you just open the door?

Highwire Acts

The first circuses, in the late eighteenth century, were shows of trick equestrianism involving amazing feats with horses and their riders. In the late nineteenth century, new acts were introduced to the circus. Still a favorite today, the flying trapeze was invented by a French gymnast at this time. His name might sound familiar. Jules Léotard gave his name to the stretchy one-piece garment still worn by many circus artists and dancers today.

49

Why are elephants wrinkled?
Would you like to try to iron one?

Why did the woman want an elephant instead of a car?
The elephant had a bigger trunk.

Ear This !

The ears of the African elephant can measure nearly 2m (6 feet) high–and can weigh almost 45 kg. (100 lbs)! They don't just look good. They help an elephant keep its cool, too. When elephants flap their ears, it helps the extra blood vessels in their ears release heat. And those big ears make good fans, too.

What did the elephant do when he broke his toe and couldn't walk?
He called a toe truck.

What do you do with a green elephant?
Wait for it to get ripe.

What's gray and squirts jam at you?
An elephant eating a doughnut.

What's large and bright purple?
An elephant holding its breath.

What has a long trunk and is found on the North Pole?
A lost elephant.

What do you get when you cross an elephant with peanut butter?
Either an elephant that sticks to the roof of your mouth or peanut butter that never forgets.

How do you hide an elephant?
Paint its tusks yellow and put it in a banana tree.

What do you give an elephant with big feet?
Lots of room.

What should you do if you see a naked elephant in a swimming pool?
Give him back his trunks.

Why can't two elephants go swimming at the same time?
They've only got one pair of trunks between them.

How does an elephant get down from a tree?
It sits on a leaf and waits for fall.

**What do elephants take
when they go away on
a long trip?**
Their trunks.

**Why do elephants paint
their toenails red?**
So they can hide in a straw-
berry patch.

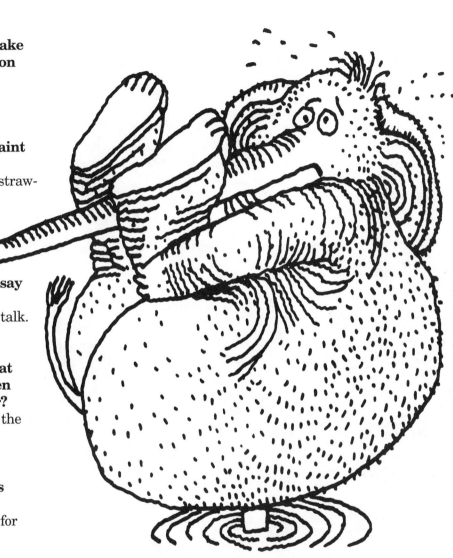

**What did the grape say
to the elephant?**
Nothing, grapes can't talk.

**How can you tell that
an elephant has been
in your refrigerator?**
Look for footprints in the
butter.

**Why can't elephants
drive cars?**
Their feet are too big for
the pedals.

**Why do elephants wear
green hats?**
So they can blend into the
crowds on St. Patrick's Day.

**Why did the elephant sit
on the marshmallow?**
It didn't want to fall into
the hot chocolate.

52

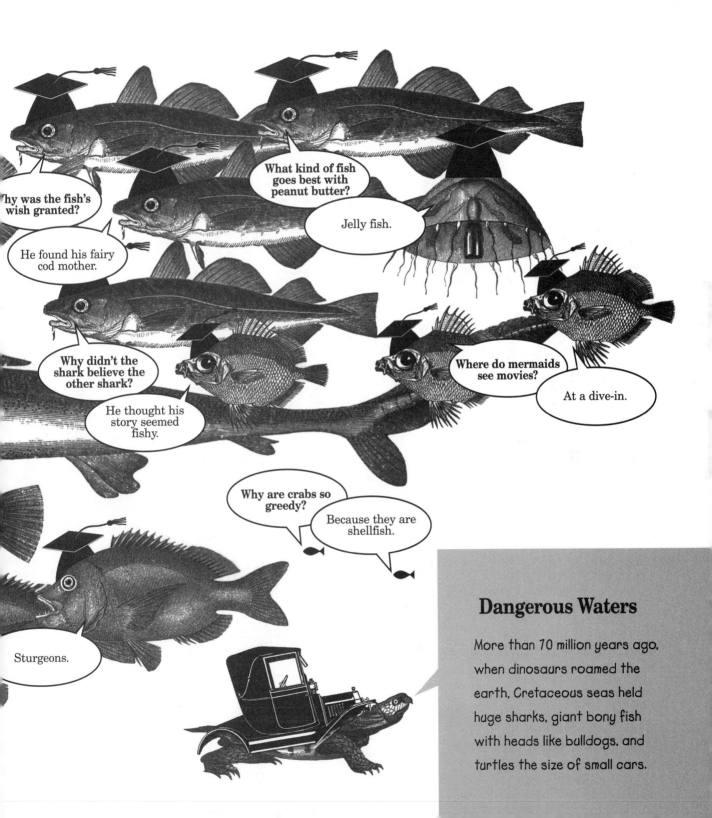

Why was the fish's wish granted?

He found his fairy cod mother.

What kind of fish goes best with peanut butter?

Jelly fish.

Why didn't the shark believe the other shark?

He thought his story seemed fishy.

Where do mermaids see movies?

At a dive-in.

Why are crabs so greedy?

Because they are shellfish.

Sturgeons.

Dangerous Waters

More than 70 million years ago, when dinosaurs roamed the earth, Cretaceous seas held huge sharks, giant bony fish with heads like bulldogs, and turtles the size of small cars.

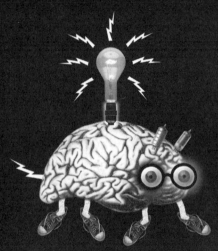

Brain Bogglers

The Jones family built a house, only to find that all four walls faced south. When they were finished building, they looked out the window and saw a bear. What color was the bear?

Mary's sister has some strange likes and dislikes. She'll buy paste but not glue; she'll eat in a deli but not a cafe; she'll ride in a cab but never a taxi. Try to figure out why she likes and dislikes these things.

Brian's mom has four children. The first was a boy named Jerry. The second was a girl named Susan. The third was a boy called Robert, and the fourth was another boy. What was his name?

Answer: White. The house must have been built on the North Pole, as this is the only point on earth where all four walls of the house could face south. Therefore, the bear was a white polar bear.

Answer: Mary's sister only likes things whose names contain two letters in alphabetical order, for example, table, paste, and deli.

Answer: Brian.

Your Amazing Brain

If all the nerve connections in one brain were placed end to end, they would be long enough to go around the earth several times! And if it were possible to convert one human brain's metabolism into energy, it would equal a 20 watt lightbulb. If all the brains in the world were converted, that would be enough energy to power around 15 big cities. Now that's brain power!

Duncan decides to take a bath and starts filling his tub. When the water reaches the top he tries to turn off the tap but it falls off. The bathroom's windows don't open and the door closes with an airtight seal. The room begins to fill up with water. Duncan can't get the door open. How does he save himself?

Uh, oh! You made Sook Yin laugh, and now everyone has the giggles. Use the clues below to figure out how long Sook Yin laughed.

- Sook Yin laughed twice as long as Patrick.
- Patrick laughed three times as long as Taryn.
- Taryn laughed as long as Emeka did.
- Emeka laughed twice as long as Jack.
- Jack laughed for half a minute.

Answer: All he has to do is pull the plug so the tub can drain.

Answer: Sook Yin laughed for 6 minutes.

57

Susan and Sheila have the same parents, look exactly alike and are the same age. But they are not twins. How is this possible?

If it takes five people one day to dig up a field, how long will it take ten people to dig up the same field?

Patty was asked how many ducks she had. She answered, "As they ran down the path, I saw one duck in front of two ducks, a duck behind two ducks, and a duck between two ducks." How many ducks did Patty have?

Answer: Susan, Sheila, and their sister Sandra are triplets.

Answer: No time at all! The field has already been dug up.

Answer: Three. The ducks were waddling down the path in single file.

A teacher left a first prize ribbon on his desk when he left the classroom. When he returned a few minutes later the ribbon was gone. He called the three students who had been in the room, and asked them if they'd seen it. The first said she'd seen it but left it where it was. The second said he'd seen it too. He said he was worried that it might blow away because the window was open, so he put it under a book on the desk. The third student said she'd seen it and was also worried that it might go missing, so she placed it between pages 53 and 54 of the book. The teacher looked, but it wasn't there. Which of the three students was lying, and how did the teacher know?

Ouch!

Have you ever wondered why it hurts when someone pulls your hair, but you don't feel anything when someone cuts it? That's because your hair that's grown out is made of dead cells. But your hair under your scalp is alive, and it's attached to nerves. When it's pulled the nerves send a "pain" message to your brain.

Answer: The third. It would be impossible to put anything between pages 53 and 54. In a book, odd pages always fall on the right and even pages on the left, so 53 and 54 couldn't be facing each other, they would be back-to-back. The student could have put the note between pages 52 and 53, or 54 and 55, but not 53 and 54.

Space Invader

Everyone has it, but yours might be different from your friend's or your brother's or sister's. What is it? Personal space. That's the space immediately around you. If someone else comes into it, it makes you feel uncomfortable. But your personal space shrinks and grows depending on whom you're with. If it's someone you trust, your personal space will be smaller. For strangers, it grows!

Can you name ten parts of the body that are spelled with only three letters?

There are two coins on the table totaling 35 cents. One of them is not a quarter. What are the coins?

A boy and his father were driving in a car during a snowstorm when the car crashed. Both were injured and had to be rushed into surgery. The surgeon walked into the boy's operating room, looked at the patient and said, "I can't operate on this boy, he's my son." How is this possible?

Answer: Here are ten body parts with three letters: Arm, leg, eye, ear, toe, rib, jaw, gum, lip, and hip.

Answer: One of them is not a quarter, but the other one is. A dime and a quarter.

Answer: The surgeon is the boy's mother.

There are six purple socks, four red socks, and eight black socks all mixed up in a drawer. The socks are exactly the same except for the color. Your room is pitch black and you have to pick out one pair of matching socks. What is the least number of socks you would have to take out of the drawer to guarantee matching a pair?

Rita lives with her parents, on the fifteenth floor of an apartment building. Each morning she takes the elevator down to the lobby, where she waits for her schoolbus. After school the schoolbus drops her off at her building. She walks back through the lobby and enters the elevator, which she takes up to the sixth floor. At the sixth floor she gets out and walks up the remaining nine flights of stairs to get to her apartment. Why doesn't she take the elevator all the way up?

Answer: Four. It would be possible to get a matching pair in the first two that you pick out, but since you can't see, you'd have to take four to guarantee a match. If you pick out a purple sock, followed by a red one, then a black sock, then the next sock you pull out, whether it's purple, red, or black, will match one of the socks already in your hand.

Answer: Rita can't reach any buttons higher than the number six.

What did the left hand say to the right hand?
How does it feel to always be right?

What did one eye say to the other?
Between you and me, something smells.

What do you lose every time you stand up?
Your lap.

What goes up but never comes down?
Your age.

What did one ear say to the other ear?
Hear! Hear!

What can you hold in your right hand but not in your left hand?
Your left elbow.

What kind of button can't you unbutton?
A belly button.

What runs but doesn't have legs?
Your nose.

Fascinating Fingernails

Bet you didn't know that your fingernails and toenails grow faster in the summer than in the winter. But all through the year fingernails grow more quickly than toenails. Nobody knows why for sure, but it may be because we use our fingers and finger-nails more than our toenails.

Doctor!
Doctor!

You didn't think we'd let you sit there and laugh without having to do any work yourself, did you? This book is filled with jokes you can entertain yourself, your friends, and your family with. Here's how to keep the fun going even after you've closed the book. With these tips under your belt, you'll be able to keep coming up with your own brilliant jokes.

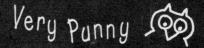 Very Punny

A lot of jokes play with words. Your English teacher would call them puns. A pun is a humorous use of a word, which can be taken as having two or more different meanings. Here are some examples:

What did the owl say when he lost his glasses?

He didn't give a hoot.

Why is a fish like someone on a diet?

They both have scales.

How do you do this on your own? Think of an object: a person, place, or thing. Then think of words that are associated with that object. Take a snake, for instance. Words associated with snakes are: slimy, poison, hiss, venom, to name a few. How about:

What's the snake's best subject at school?

Hiss-tory.

How to Make Your Own Jokes

Words that Sound Similar

Words that sound similar to other words but have a different meaning can make clever jokes—like Knock! Knock! jokes. All you have to do is think of a name or an object and think of a word it sounds like. For instance:

Knock! Knock!
Who's there?
Al.
Al who?
Al be happy when you open the door and let me in.

And here's an example of a rhyming word joke:

What was the owl's favorite TV show?
The feather forecast.

Say What?

Putting together two things that don't usually go together in one joke can make us laugh. Just think of two things you wouldn't associate with each other—for example, a frog and a bicycle—and characteristics of each.

It doesn't have to make sense (in fact, it shouldn't!). You could come up with:

What's green and slimy and has two wheels?
A frog riding a bicycle.

And here's another:

What has red hair and 100 legs?
A centipede wearing a wig.

After telling a few jokes like the absurd ones above, you can "trick" people by saying something true or obvious that's not the answer they're expecting to a joke. Here are a few examples, including the most famous one:

Why did the chicken cross the road? To get to the other side.

Why did the boy on stilts pick up the phone? Because it was ringing.

What did the cat say to the spider? Nothing. Cats can't talk.

What's at the end of the rainbow?

The other end of the rainbow. Although rainbows look like arcs, they are actually round, forming a colored light ring opposite the sun. They seem like arcs because most of the time the bottom half is blocked by the horizon so we only see part of the rainbow.

Can February March?
No, but April May.

Why was 6 afraid of 7?
Because 7 8 9.

What gets wetter the more you dry?
A towel.

Why do you have to be careful with sunrises and sunsets?
Because day breaks and night falls.

Which kind of house weighs the least?
A lighthouse.

What's full of holes but holds water?
A sponge.

What are two things you can't eat for breakfast?
Lunch and dinner.

What's round and bad-tempered?
A vicious circle.

Why did the judge send the turtle to jail?
Because he was known as a hard case.

Have you heard the joke about the jump rope?
Skip it.

Why are pianos hard to open?
Because the keys don't open locks.

Why is a slippery sidewalk like music?
If you don't C Sharp, you'll B Flat.

What works only after it's been fired?
A rocket.

Which month of the year has 26 days?
All of them.

How many books can you carry in an empty backpack?
None. The backpack's empty!

What can you put into a barrel full of water to make it lighter?
A hole.

A Bear-Sized Nap

Grizzly and black bears dig dens in the fall and then go into a dormant period, like hibernation, for 4 to 7 months over the winter. They spend this time in their dens and usually don't eat, urinate, or defecate until they go back out in the spring.

71

"A Swell Affair"

To brush or not to brush

Nylon toothbrushes, like the one you use every day, weren't invented until 1938. That doesn't mean that people only started brushing their teeth then. Toothbrushes were actually invented around the late 1400s in China and were made out of animal hair, such as pig bristles.

When do dentists get angry?
When they run out of patients.

Alexander the Great   Bozo the Clown

Why did the farmer drive a steamroller over her potato field?
So she could grow squash instead.

What does a farmer grow if he works very hard?
Tired.

Why did the nurse tiptoe past the medicine cabinet?
He didn't want to wake the sleeping pills.

What did the electrician say when she looked at the fuse box?
Nothing, she was too shocked.

Why did the scientist invent a better lightbulb?
She had a bright idea.

Why did the scientist put a knocker on his door?
He wanted to win the no bell prize.

Why did the tap dancer retire?
She kept falling into the sink.

Why do candle-makers only work two days a week?
They only work on wick-ends.

Why did the man put a clock under his desk?
He wanted to work over time.

Why did the robber take a shower?
He wanted to make a clean getaway.

A butcher is six feet tall. What does he weigh?
Meat.

Why did the sailor drop to the floor?
The captain called "All hands on deck."

Cowabunga!

How many stomachs does a cow have? Only one, just like we do, except there are four compartments in a cow's stomach. These come in handy because, on average, a cow eats about 36 kgs (80 lbs.) of food a day!

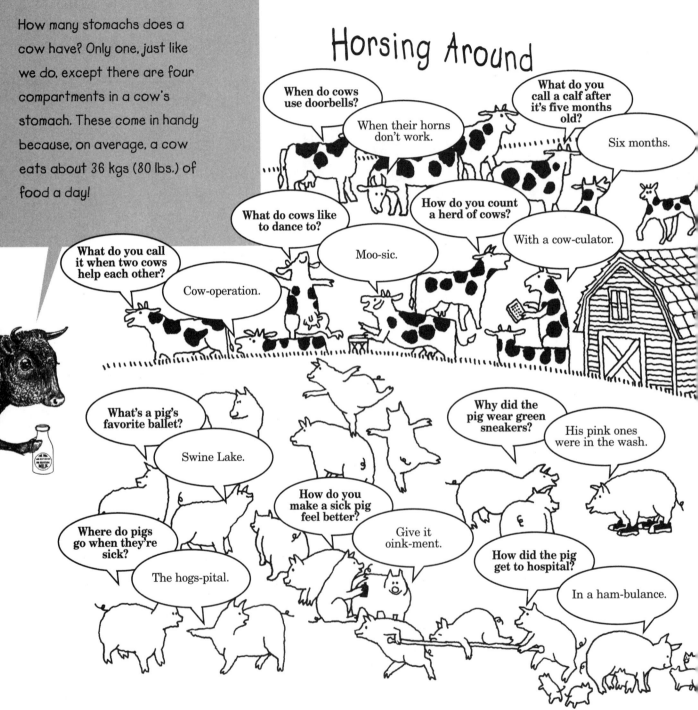

Horsing Around

When do cows use doorbells?

When their horns don't work.

What do you call a calf after it's five months old?

Six months.

What do cows like to dance to?

Moo-sic.

How do you count a herd of cows?

With a cow-culator.

What do you call it when two cows help each other?

Cow-operation.

What's a pig's favorite ballet?

Swine Lake.

Why did the pig wear green sneakers?

His pink ones were in the wash.

Where do pigs go when they're sick?

The hogs-pital.

How do you make a sick pig feel better?

Give it oink-ment.

How did the pig get to hospital?

In a ham-bulance.

75

Why did the chicken cross the road?
To get to the other side.

Why did the computer cross the road?
To get to the other site.

Why did the cow cross the road?
To see the udder side.

Why did the cows cross the road?
To get to the moo-vies.

Why did the chicken only cross to the center of the road?
It wanted to lay it on the line.

Why did the dinosaur cross the road?
Because he wasn't a chicken.

Why did the *T-rex* cross the road?
Because chickens hadn't evolved yet.

Why did the giraffe cross the road?
Because the chicken wasn't around.

Optical Illusions

Standing Sticks ▶

Turn the book slightly,
so the corner is in front
of you, and look at the
lines in the direction of
the arrow. Now tip it
slightly away from you.
What happens when
you close one eye and
look at the lines? Do the
lines look like they are
standing straight up off
the page?

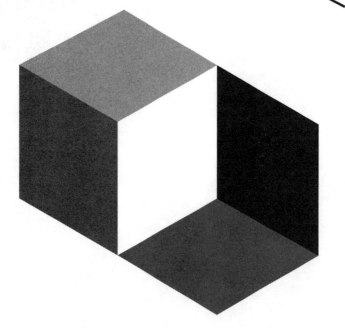

◀ One cube or two?

There are two cubes
in the picture at left,
but you can only see
one cube at a time.
Which one you see all
depends on which
corner of the white
side your brain thinks
is closer to you. Which
cube do you see first?

◀ Floating Balls

What happens when you stare at this picture for a few seconds? The balls come to life. The light-colored balls seem to rise up from the page. The shadow beneath makes this more realistic by giving the balls depth.

Face to Face ▶

Look at the dot in this box. Is it at the front of the cube or at the back? Are you sure?

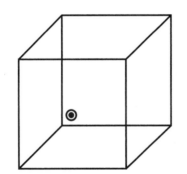

1961

An Unusual Year

The year 1961 has an unusual distinction. Have you figured out what that is? Hint: Turn the book so you can look at this page upside down. What you'll discover is that 1961 upside down is still 1961! We'll have to wait a very, very long time until that happens again. The next time this will be true will be in the year 6009.

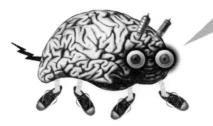

Which central circle is larger, the one on the left or the one on the right? You may have guessed the right answer already. They're the same size. The perspective just changes with the size of the other shapes that surround the central circle.

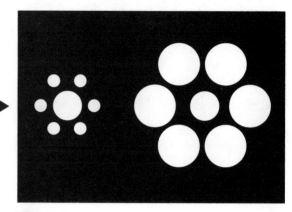

Are the horizontal lines parallel? Believe it or not, they are. You can test them with a ruler or another straight edge.

Study this figure for a few seconds. What do you see? A white vase, or two black faces?

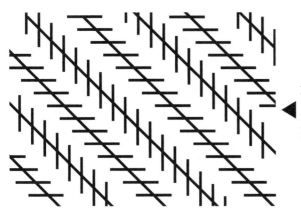

Are the longer diagonal lines parallel? Yes, indeed. Those smaller lines drawn across are just trying to make our brains believe otherwise.

Look closely at the square. Do the lines appear to be wavy? By now you know not to be fooled by appearances. Your trusty ruler will show you that the lines of the square are all straight. The background lines put a different twist on things, though.

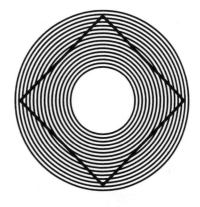

Lefty or Righty?

Nine people out of ten are right-handed. And some people—but very few—are ambidextrous (that means they can use either hand to do the same task). Other people are mixed-handed, meaning they can do different tasks with different hands.

Which image is on top? Most people see this image as two triangles, one on top of the other, because the triangle is such a familiar shape. Very few people see this as two shapes that are side by side. How do you see it?

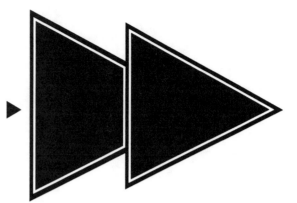

Do you see birds or bunnies, or both?

Is this book opening away from you or toward you? Does it keep changing?

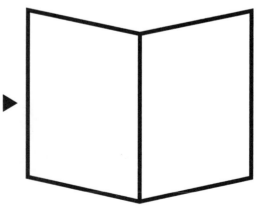

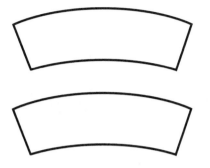

Which of these objects is larger? Actually, they are the same size. The shape on top just looks smaller because its shorter arc is next to the longer arc of the lower figure.

Do you see a triangle in this shape? The shape cut into the circles "tricks" our eye into seeing a triangle here, when in fact there isn't one drawn.

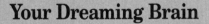

Your Dreaming Brain

Scientists who study brain activity during sleep believe that dreams happen in the right hemisphere of our brains. The left hemisphere is our verbal side. When people say they don't dream, what they really mean is that they don't remember their dreams. Everyone dreams. It just depends from individual to individual whether we are able to transfer the right brain images to the verbal left brain.

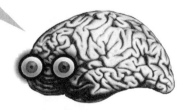

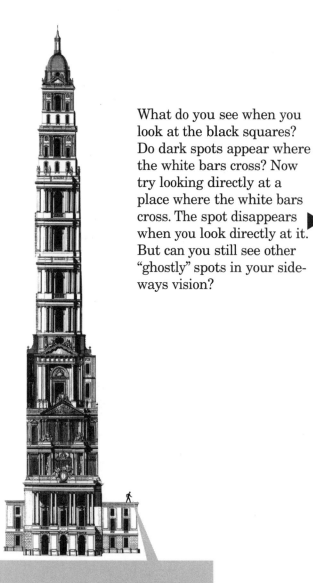

What do you see when you look at the black squares? Do dark spots appear where the white bars cross? Now try looking directly at a place where the white bars cross. The spot disappears when you look directly at it. But can you still see other "ghostly" spots in your sideways vision? ▶

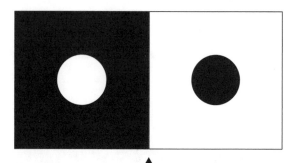

▲

Which circle is bigger, the white one or the black one? If you guessed the white circle you wouldn't be alone. But, you'd actually be wrong. Believe it or not, they're exactly the same size!

How High Is High?

Though these are still only ideas, today's engineers say that within the next 100 years, we will see buildings that are 250 to 500 stories tall! That could be an awfully long elevator ride to the top.

This strange-looking object is called a **blivit**. Look at it carefully. Where is the middle prong attached?

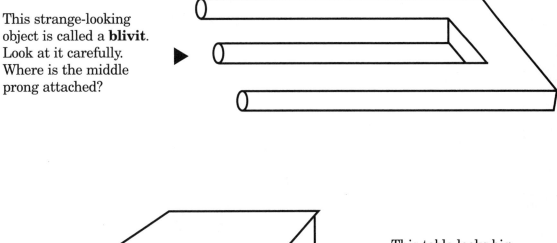

This table looks big enough to hold a penny, or does it? Can you fit a penny on this drawing without the coin touching any of the lines?

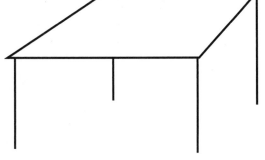

Which line is longer, the top or the bottom one? Although most people would say the bottom line looks longer, they're—you guessed it—the exact same length!

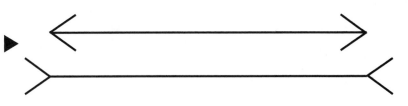

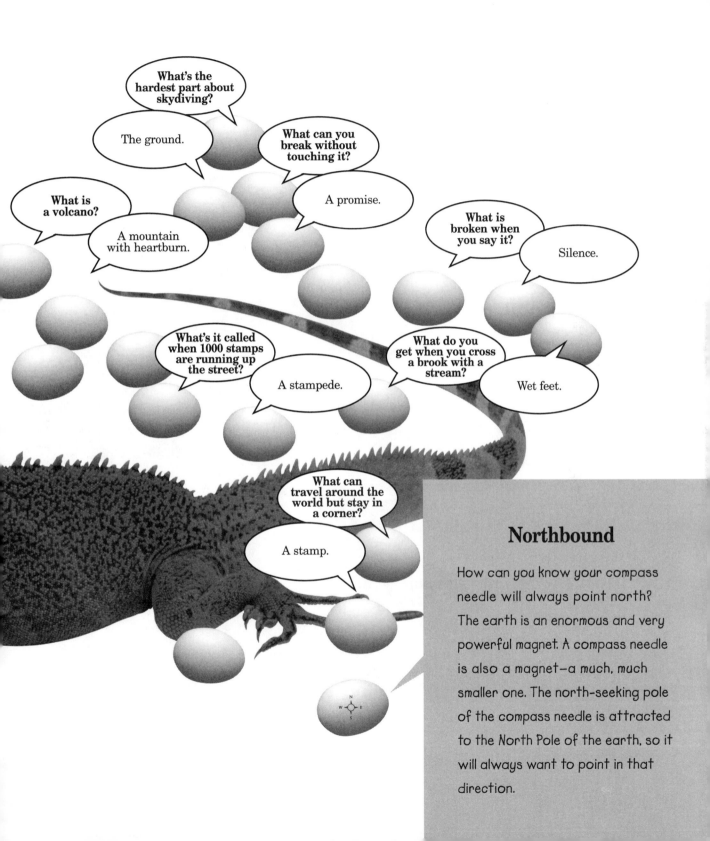

Northbound

How can you know your compass needle will always point north? The earth is an enormous and very powerful magnet. A compass needle is also a magnet—a much, much smaller one. The north-seeking pole of the compass needle is attracted to the North Pole of the earth, so it will always want to point in that direction.

88

Climbing Cat

In 1950 a four-month-old kitten followed mountaineers to the top of the Matterhorn in the Alps. It climbed the 4,000 m (14,000 feet) in stages, but got a break on the way down when it hitched a ride in a mountain guide's backpack.

Why can't you play games in the jungle?
Because there's always gonna be a cheetah.

What has stripes and sixteen wheels?
A zebra wearing roller skates.

What's black and white and eats like a horse?
A zebra.

What monkey is always exploding?
A ba-boom.

What do snakes do after a fight?
Hiss and make up.

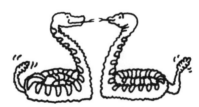

What's a monkey's favorite Christmas song?
Jungle bells.

What do you call a hippopotamus with the measles?

A hippo-spotty-mus.

Why can't you play jokes on snakes?
You can't pull their legs!

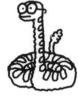

What do you do if a six-ton gorilla tells you a joke?
You laugh ...very loudly!

Why do lions eat raw meat?
They don't know how to cook.

What do you call a lion that's eaten your dad's sister?
An aunt-eater.

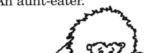

Drooling Crocs!

Have you ever looked closely at a crocodile's jaws? Probably not . . . or you wouldn't be here to read this! But if you examine a photograph of a crocodile, you'll see that they have huge mouths and lots of teeth, but they don't have any lips. Without lips to seal them shut, their mouths leak when they're closed. How embarrassing!

What's invisible and smells like banana?
A gorilla's burp.

How do you stop a cobra from striking?

unfair

Pay it a decent wage.

mOre $

Why do gorillas have such large nostrils?
Because they have such big fingers.

Fluffy's Nine Lives

Cats have had a colorful history. Ancient Egyptians worshipped them. They even mummified cats when they died—the same honor bestowed on Pharaohs. By the second century, cats had become popular in Europe as well. But around 1300, trouble started for the cat. People came to believe that cats were associated with evil and witches. Soon cats were almost extinct in Europe. Then the Black Death plague struck. Borne by disease-carrying rats, this devasting disease rapidly spread across the continent. Millions of people died. Luckily for our feline friends, people saw how valuable cats are when it comes to keeping down the rodent population. Seems like cats have earned their current status as beloved household pets.

Animals Just Want to Have Fun

Like us, animals seem to like to play and have fun, especially baby animals. Scientists believe that aside from sheer enjoyment, playing together is a form of bonding with their fellow animals. Also, some kinds of play help young animals to grow strong and to learn important survival skills, such as pouncing on prey to become good hunters.

Animal Facts

Animal Phrases

We use animal phrases, like "it's raining cats and dogs," all the time. Here are two more:

GET YOUR GOAT! If someone is making you angry, you might say they are "getting your goat." Actually, it originally was "get your goad." A goad is a cattle prod, used to poke animals to make them hurry up or move.

HAPPY AS A CLAM. When something great happens to you, you feel "happy as a clam." The original phrase is actually "happy as a clam at high tide." Since clam diggers can only wade into the seawater and dig for clams in the sand at low tide, clams are happy and safe from capture at high tide.

Woof? Woof?

Everybody knows that when a dog barks it says Woof! Right? Well, not exactly. A French dog would probably sound the same to you as an English one does, but the way the noises are written in different languages can be fun to look at. A Russian dog, for instance, says Gaf! And a Czech dog says Haf! In Finland, dogs say How! And in Denmark it's Vov! Here are some other animal sounds:

	ENGLISH	FRENCH	SPANISH
DOG	Woof!	Oua!	Gauff!
CAT	Meow!	Miaou!	Miau!
COW	Moo!	Meu!	Moou!

Moou!

You speak Spanish well.

Mooo-chas gracias!

What did the violin say to the musician?

Stop picking on me.

Which band member is most likely to be struck by lightning?
The conductor.

Why did the DJ put an old shoe in his ear?
He liked to listen to sole music.

What kind of music does your father like to sing?
Pop music.

Did you hear the one about the musician who wrote all his music in bed?
He insisted on writing sheet music.

Which composer runs around castles?
Moat-zart.

How does the sky listen to music?
Through the cloud-speaker.

How do you make a bandstand?
Take their chairs away.

What keeps jazz musicians on earth?
Groovity.

Making Music

Did you know that Beethoven, who composed some of the world's best-loved music, was deaf? He used to cut the legs off his pianos so he could "hear" what he was playing by feeling the vibrations the music made through the floor.

Riddles

1

Who is this person? It is not my sister, nor my brother, but it is a child of my father and mother.

2

If your aunt's brother is not your uncle, then who is he?

3

Who is your father's sister's sister-in-law?

4

I have eyes but cannot see. I have ears but cannot hear. I have lips but cannot speak. I will always look the same. Nothing will ever change me. What am I?

5

I have lived one year. I have lived hundreds of years. I am seen in nearly every part of the world. I live near mountains, near the sea, near the roads and plains. I am a life force. Without me the world will be bare.

6

What doesn't get any wetter no matter how much it rains?

7

If a cat can jump 5 feet in the air, then why can't it jump through a 2-foot high window?

8

What has a mouth but doesn't eat, a bank without money, a bed but doesn't sleep, and waves but has no hands?

9

David's father has three sons: Snap, Crackle and_____?

10

You're a bus driver on your bus route. At the first stop, three girls with blonde hair get on, while a man eating an ice cream cone gets off. At the second stop, five boys who just won their baseball game, and a woman with a yellow-polka-dot dress pay the fee and enter the bus; nobody gets off. At the third stop, a man carrying a monkey exits the bus. Nobody new joins the ride. What's the bus driver's name?

11

A bus driver is going up a one-way street the wrong way. Halfway down the street he gets spotted by a police officer, and waves hello to him. If the bus driver is going down a one-way street the wrong way, why does the police officer not pull him over and give him a ticket?

What's a boxer's favorite drink?
Punch.

What kind of socks do baseball players wear?
Ones with runs in them.

Why are basketball players sloppy eaters?
They're always dribbling.

Which football player wears the biggest shoes?
The one with the biggest feet.

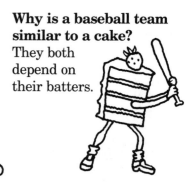

Size 18

Why does it get hot after a baseball game?
All the fans have left.

Why did the football coach go to the bank?
He wanted to get his quarter back.

Why is tennis such a noisy game?
Each player raises a racquet.

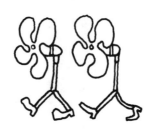

Why is a baseball team similar to a cake?
They both depend on their batters.

Why do basketball players have long arms?
If their arms were any shorter they wouldn't reach their hands.

What can be served but not eaten?
A tennis ball.

What is a football player's favorite drink?

Penal-tea.

How are tennis players like judges?
They spend a lot of time at the court.

Why do soccer players do so well in math?
They know how to use their heads.

How do hockey players greet each other?
By "hi" sticking.

What letter does golf start with?
A tee.

Take Heart

In an average week, assuming you exercise, your heart will beat about 1 million times. When it's very active, your heart can pump about 75 litres (20 gallons) of blood each minute. That's enough to fill a bathtub every 2 minutes!

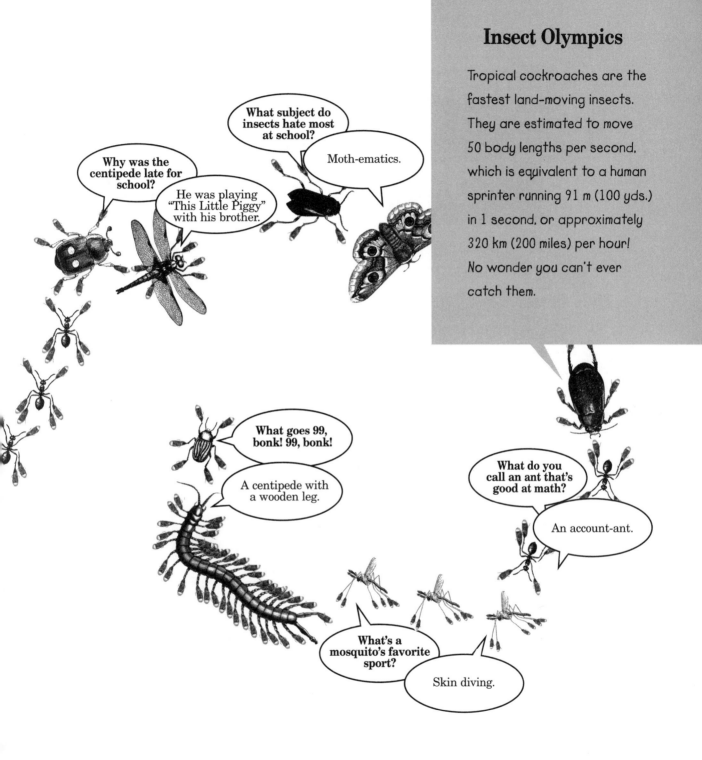

Insect Olympics

Tropical cockroaches are the fastest land-moving insects. They are estimated to move 50 body lengths per second, which is equivalent to a human sprinter running 91 m (100 yds.) in 1 second, or approximately 320 km (200 miles) per hour! No wonder you can't ever catch them.

Why was the centipede late for school?

He was playing "This Little Piggy" with his brother.

What subject do insects hate most at school?

Moth-ematics.

What goes 99, bonk! 99, bonk!

A centipede with a wooden leg.

What do you call an ant that's good at math?

An account-ant.

What's a mosquito's favorite sport?

Skin diving.

Visual Games

1.

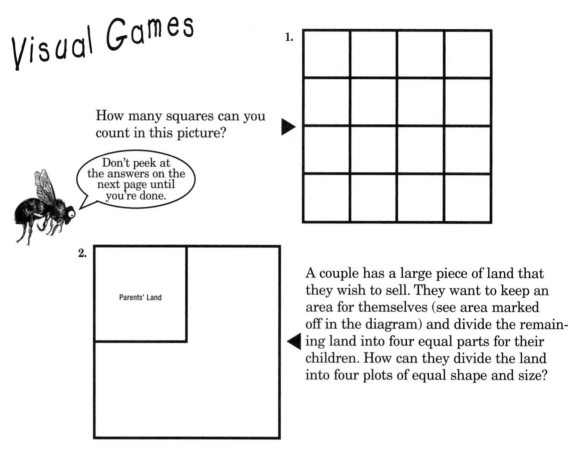

How many squares can you count in this picture?

Don't peek at the answers on the next page until you're done.

2.

Parents' Land

A couple has a large piece of land that they wish to sell. They want to keep an area for themselves (see area marked off in the diagram) and divide the remaining land into four equal parts for their children. How can they divide the land into four plots of equal shape and size?

Can you make this pyramid of buttons turn upside down by moving only three buttons? Hint: You might want to collect 10 coins or buttons and build this shape to try out different options if you're having difficulty figuring it out just in your head.

3.

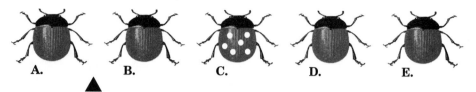

A. B. C. D. E.

Can you "spot" the ladybugs? Using the following 3 clues, you should be able to figure out how many spots each ladybug has.

1. If a ladybug has an even number of spots, then the one to her right will have 1 more spot than she has.
2. If a ladybug has an odd number of spots, then the 1 to her right will have 3 more spots than she has.
3. Each ladybug has at least 1 spot.

Copy these 2 arrows onto another piece of paper. Then, using only 2 straight lines, can you make a third arrow.

You'll need 12 matches or straws for this puzzle. Set them up like this. By moving only 3 matches or straws, can you make 3 equal squares?

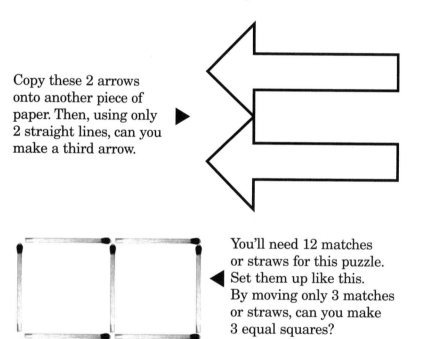

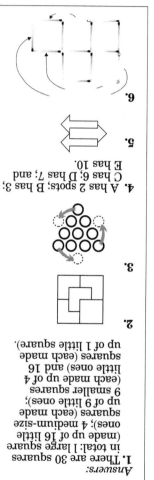

104

Have an Ice Day

There's nothing like reaching into your refrigerator on a hot day to take out a cool drink. And think of all the food in there that would go bad if it were left out. But what did people do before there were fridges to keep food cold and fresh? Imagine walking up to the top of a mountain to lug snow and ice home to use as your refrigerator. That's what the ancient Greeks and Romans did. They dug holes in the ground, lined them with logs and straw, packed in snow and ice, and covered them up. Believe it or not, the ice and snow compressed and stayed frozen for months.

Why couldn't the dessert reach the table?
It was shortbread.

What kind of sandwiches do sailors eat?
Submarines, of course!

What kind of cup can't hold water?
A cupcake.

What do you get when you cross peanut butter and a quilt?
A bread spread.

What did the banana do when the lion roared at it?
It split.

What did the baby corn say to Ma Corn?
Where's Pop Corn?

When does a potato change nationality?
When it's French-fried.

What do you call a green vegetable served on a ship?
A crew-cumber.

The Croc Diet

Up to 60% of a crocodile's food intake can be converted to fat. This makes it able to go a long time between meals. In fact, some large crocodiles have been known to be able to survive up to two years between meals.

If Jack and Jill were a fruit what kind would they be?
A pear.

Why did the tomato go out with the zucchini?
Because he couldn't find a date.

What do you call two banana skins?
Slippers.

Why did the oak tree eat his ice cream out of a dish?
Because the pine tree wouldn't give him a cone.

What's a plumber's favorite vegetable?
Leeks.

What do you call a necklace made of fruit?
A food chain.

A cabbage, a tap, and a tomato were in a race. What happened?
The cabbage was ahead, but the tap kept running, and the tomato was trying to ketchup.

What would you have if you had 18 watermelons, 87 pears, 65 lemons, and 971 grapes?

A fruit store.

Knock! Knock!
Who's there?
Comb.
Comb who?
Comb over and see my new puppy.

Knock! Knock!
Who's there?
Bean.
Bean who?
Bean anywhere nice lately?

Knock! Knock!
Who's there?
Penny.
Penny who?
Penny for your thoughts.

Knock! Knock!
Who's there?
Peek.
Peek who?
Peek-a-boo.

Knock! Knock!
Who's there?
Jigsaw.
Jigsaw who?
Jigsaw you peeping through the window.

Knock! Knock!
Who's there?
Jess.
Jess who?
Jess me and my shadow.

Knock! Knock!
Who's there?
Yolanda.
Yolanda who?
Yolanda me some money?

Knock! Knock!
Who's there?
Kent.
Kent who?
Kent you tell by my voice?

Knock! Knock!
Who's there?
Hans.
Hans who?
Hans off the TV remote control, I'm watching this show.

Knock! Knock!
Who's there?
Ben.
Ben who?
Ben knocking on your door all afternoon!

Knock! Knock!
Who's there?
Hutch.
Hutch who?
Bless you!

Knock! Knock!
Who's there?
Eileen.
Eileen who?
Eileen over to tie my shoe!

Knock! Knock!
Who's there?
Olive.
Olive who?
Olive you! How do you feel about me?

Knock! Knock!
Who's there?
Justin.
Justin who?
Justin case you were wondering.

Knock! Knock!
Who's there?
Justin.
Justin who?
Justin time for dinner!

Knock! Knock!
Who's there?
Les.
Les who?
Les go for a swim!

Knock! Knock!
Who's there?
Sarah.
Sarah who?
Sarah doctor in the house?

Knock! Knock!
Who's there?
Nobody.
If nobody's there, then who's telling the joke?

By the sea

What is a shrimp's favorite place to shop?
At a prawn-shop.

What did the crab buy at the bakery?
Chocolate e-claws.

Why are fishermen like mad dogs?
They always want a bite.

What's the best way to catch a fish?
Have someone throw it to you.

What part of the fish weighs the most?
The scales.

Why is the sea salty?
Because fish don't like pepper.

How does the sea greet the sand?
It waves.

What's the difference between the earth and the sea?
The earth is dirty, but the sea is tide-y.

Why does the ocean roar?
You would too if you had sharks in your bed!

Which is the best day to go to the beach?
Sun-day.

What can fall on the sea without getting wet?
Your shadow.

What kind of bed does a mermaid sleep in?
A water bed.

When is a boat not a boat?
When it's a-float.

What washes up on small beaches?
Micro-waves.

A Whale of a Size!

Blue whales are the largest animals in the world. An average male is as long as a basketball court—and the females are bigger. Even newborn blue whales weigh as much as a full-grown Indian elephant!

Surely You Jest

What people think is funny has changed a lot over time, but one thing's for sure: comedy itself has been around a long, long time. The first stand-up comedians came on the scene about 4,500 years ago to entertain the Egyptian Pharaohs. English and French kings, around 500–1,000 years ago, kept court comedians, called "fools" or "jesters." They were often treated poorly. They were usually dwarves, often deformed people, who were paid to dress up and entertain at banquets with their pranks and amusing chatter. Although these jesters were thought to not be very intelligent people, in fact their position often allowed them to make outrageous and rude comments to kings, queens and Pharaohs that other "servants" wouldn't dare.

Laughter... Pass it on

Sometimes you don't even have to know what's funny to enjoy the benefits of a good laugh. Have you ever been around friends and someone starts laughing, then another person, and even though you don't know what they are laughing about you start laughing too? Sometimes it can take ages to stop. Even if you never find out what started the giggle session, you'll feel great after.

 More Laugh Facts

Sad to Glad

Usually we laugh because something's funny, but laughter is also a tension-release mechanism to help us feel better if we're in an uncomfortable situation. Say your teacher asks you a question in front of the whole class and you draw a complete blank. You might laugh when you don't know the answer, but not because you really think it's funny. In fact, you may feel pretty embarrassed. But laughing helps you get rid of some of your tension. Laughing sensors in your body send signals to your brain, activating neurons that tell you that you feel good.

You Think that's Funny?

Imagine this: your baby brother comes into your room and knocks over a model you've been working on. Because of his age and lack of experience he may find it very funny that bits and pieces of your work go flying all over the room. He's just not old enough to understand. Or, you might hear an adult roar with laughter about something that you don't find at all funny. Things like which country we come from, how we are raised, and our ages all contribute to what we find funny.

What do you call ants that live in apartments?

Ten-ants.

What do you call a fly with no wings?

A walk.

What do you call a mosquito in a tin suit?

A bite in shining armor.

How does a flea travel so fast?

By itch-hiking.

What lies on its back, one hundred feet in the air?

A dead centipede.

Mosquito's Best Friend

Do mosquitoes think you're particularly tasty? Some people believe that mosquitoes are more attracted to some people's blood than others. One theory is that it might have something to do with the amount of carbon dioxide a person's skin releases. Others believe it's the warmth and wetness of the skin that's appealing. And there are those who believe that everyone gets bitten equally, but not everyone reacts the same way.

Monster
Mania

Are You My Mummy?

Mummies aren't found only in Egypt. They're all over the world. In an Italian city called Palermo, for instance, there's an underground city of the dead that has about 6,000 bodies all amazingly well preserved by the cool, dry underground air. Over 100 years ago, when people died, their bodies were laid out on shelves in the clothes they were buried in. People who lived in Palermo would go down to the catacombs to pay respects to their dead relatives.

Where is ghosts' mail delivered?
The ghost office.

What does the ghost read every day?
His horror-scope.

What's the scariest ride at the amusement park?
The roller-ghoster.

What do ghosts eat for dinner?
Spook-ghetti.

Why did the 1000-year-old Egyptian go on the school field trip?
She heard that the mummies and daddies were invited, too.

Why did the mummy keep his bandages in the refrigerator?
He wanted to use them for cold cuts.

What happened when the toddler mummy told a lie?
He was sent to his tomb.

What does a witch order when she stays in a hotel?
Broom service.

Is it true that witches are afraid of dead bodies?
Of corpse it is.

How do you make a witch itch?
Take out the W.

What do you get when you cross a snowman with a vampire?
Frost-bite.

What do you call twin boy vampires?
Blood brothers!

What do you say to a skeleton going on vacation?
Bone voyage!

Why do elves get indigestion?
They keep goblin their food.

What do you get when you cross a cow with a werewolf?
A steak that bites back!

What's a monster's favorite cheese?
Monster-ella.

What do you call a 10-foot monster?
Shorty.

How can you tell if a Martian is a good gardener?
It has a green thumb.

What kind of coffee does a vampire drink?
De-coffin-ated.

What do you get when a ghost sits on a branch?
Petrified wood.

What's a monster baby's favorite drink?
Ghoul-ade.

What did one ghost say to the other?
Don't spook until you're spooken to!

What's Dracula's favorite fruit?
Neck-tarine.

What's a ghost's favorite dessert?
Boo-berries and I-scream.

What kind of mistakes do ghosts make?
Boo-boos.

What do you call a witch that lives on the beach?
A sand-witch.

What's a vampire's favorite boat?
A blood vessel.

What do sea monsters eat for dinner?

Potato ships.

Why's the vampire so unpopular?
He's a pain-in-the-neck.

Who was the monster's date for the prom?
His ghoul-friend.

What type of dog do vampires have?
Blood hounds.

Why didn't the skeleton go to the party?
Because no body would go with him.

How do you know when a monster has a cold?
He starts coffin.

What do vampires take for bad colds?
Coffin drops.

Why do skeletons play the piano?
Because they don't have organs.

A Dose of Blood

Some scientists believe that back in the middle ages "vampires" were just sick people who had an incurable genetic disease called porphyria. This disease had unpleasant physical effects, such as the inability to tolerate sunlight. Back then they believed that drinking enough blood might help cure their symptoms.

What has webbed feet and wants to suck your blood?
Count Quack-ula.

What's big, green, and can't stop crying?
The Incredible Sulk.

What do vampires say after they have eaten?
Fang-you very much.

What was written on the robot's tombstone?
Rust in peace.

What do you call a cat that's a ghost?
A scaredy-cat.

What room doesn't have a ghost in it?
A living room.

How can you tell when a mummy is angry?
It flips its lid.

What happened when the girl ghost met the boy ghost?
It was love at first fright.

What did the ghost have for lunch?
Grave-y.

What Big Eyes You've Got!

Real monsters lurk in the depths of the ocean. Although rarely seen, sometimes giant squids get caught in fishing nets or wash up on shore so we can get a close-up view of these gigantic creatures. Their eyes alone are the size of a car's hubcaps—the largest eyes in the world!

Going My Way?

Around 100 million waterfowl migrate from Canada to the warmer climates of the southern United States and Central and South America each fall. Scientists know that many different waterfowl use the same four major "flyroutes" to head south for the winter. Although they don't know exactly how these birds find their way, scientists believe that some of these routes have been used for more than a million years!

What bird is always in the kitchen?

A cook-oo.

What bird can write under water?

A ball-point pen-guin.

What did the cuckoo say when it fell off a branch?

Cuck-plop.

What kind of movies do ducks like best?

Duck-umentaries.

Why do birds fly south in the winter?

It's a pretty long way to walk.

124

Knock! Knock!
Who's there?
A little kid.
A little kid who?
A little kid who can't reach the doorbell!

Knock! Knock!
Who's there?
Abbot.
Abbot who?
Abbot you don't know who this is.

Knock! Knock!
Who's there?
Adore.
Adore who?
Adore is between us, open up!

Will you remember me in 10 years?
Yes.
Will you remember me next year?
Yes.
Will you remember me next month?
Yes.
Will you remember me next week?
Yes.
Will you remember me in a minute?
Yes.
Knock! Knock!
Who's there?
I thought you said you'd remember me.

Knock! Knock!
Who's there?
Radio.
Radio who?
Radio not, here I come.

Knock! Knock!
Who's there?
Alison.
Alison who?
Alison to the radio every night when I'm falling asleep.

Knock! Knock!
Who's there?
Dwayne.
Dwayne who?
Dwayne the bathtub, I'm dwowning!

Knock! Knock!
Who's there?
Zombies.
Zombies who?
Zombies make honey, zombies just buzz around.

Knock! Knock!
Who's there?
Canoe.
Canoe who?
Canoe open the door?

Knock! Knock!
Who's there?
Cow.
Cow who?
Cow are you doing?

Knock! Knock!
Who's there?
Alex.
Alex who?
Alex plain later, just let me in.

Knock! Knock!
Who's there?
Barry.
Barry who?
Barry nice to meet you.

Knock! Knock!
Who's there?
Russian.
Russian who?
Russian around all day to get here on time.

Knock! Knock!
Who's there?
Howard!
Howard who?
Howard you like to go and get an ice cream?

Knock! Knock!
Who's there?
Noah.
Noah who?
Noah more jokes.

Knock! Knock!
Go away!

Knock! Knock!
Who's there?
Ima.
Ima who?
Ima not lying.
That was it. There aren't any more jokes.
Please stop knocking.

Knock! Knock!
Who's there?
I.
I who?
I have been very patient.
Now close the book.
The jokes are done.
Finished.
Over.
You have to move on.